P9-DHB-457

Ballesteros on My Mind

My Hometown in the Philippines

Written by
Rey E. de la Cruz

Illustrated by
Tenni Magcase

Text copyright © 2016 by Rey E. de la Cruz
Illustrations copyright © 2016 by Tenni Magcase

All rights reserved. No part of this book may be reproduced, transmitted, or stored in an information-retrieval system in any form or by any means electronic, mechanical, photocopying, recording, or otherwise, without written permission from the author or publisher.

LCCN: 2016937106
ISBN: 978-0-9964694-4-9

Book design: Tenni Magcase
Layout design: Syd Lopez

The illustrations are rendered in watercolor, colored pencils, and art markers on 140 lbs. watercolor paper.

The production staff of the book trailers:
Director and animator: Sandie Oreta Gillis
Assistant director: Ivan Kevin R. Castro
Narrators: Jack Leander Imperial and Raphael B. Mallabo

Second Printing, 2017

Carayan Press
P.O. Box 31816
San Francisco, California 94131-0816, U.S.A.
Email: carayan@carayanpress.com
www. carayanpress.com

Printed in the U.S.A.

Ballesteros on My Mind
My Hometown in the Philippines

To Daddy, Mommy, Elmer, Oscar, Vilma, and my townmates in Ballesteros, Cagayan—R.E.D.

For my beloved Melvyn Patrick Lopez, who continues to inspire me from the stars—tenni M

Acknowledgments

Emmanuel C. Baccaray, Rodina B. Baccaray, Merlita T. Bayuga, Orlando P. Bernardino
Merlita Usita Campañano, Ivan Kevin R. Castro, Leo T. Centeno, Joe S. Collado,
Wyrlo D. Edrozo Sr., Margaret A. Fashing, Penelope V. Flores, Ph.D.,
Almira Astudillo Gilles, Ph.D., Sandie Oreta Gillis, Alvin Mark G. Hipolito,
Jack Leander Imperial, Syd Lopez, Angioline A. Loredo,
Edwin A. Lozada, Raphael B. Mallabo, Gia R. Mendoza,
Eleanor S. Modesto, Rachel Edrozo Onza, Nancy Oandasan Pascua,
Nora Edrozo Rasos, Donna J. Rohrlack, Maria Teresita B. Sindiong,
Rene R. Sixtos, Nimfa Alvarez Sta. Ana, Mary Jane A. Tancinco,
Pat Whitson-Kane, Yvonne Liu Wolf, and Lizzie Eder Zobel.

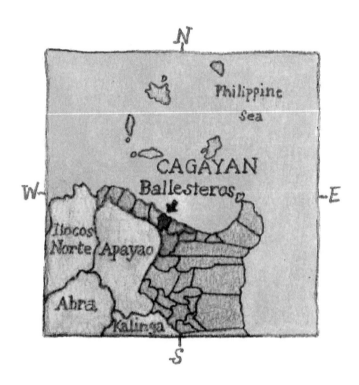

No matter where our feet take us, our hearts and minds remain in a place we call home. Rey E. de la Cruz's heartwarming book about his hometown in the Philippines captures the universal longing for that special place.

In 1957, when I was three years old, my family moved to Ballesteros. My father was an army officer who was assigned to different places. He and my mother decided that we leave the city and live in their hometown, Ballesteros.

My mother, who worked as a nurse in the city, stayed home and took care of my two brothers, a sister, and me. She took up gardening as a hobby, and earned money growing and selling bougainvilleas.

The Philippines has 7,100 islands, of which Luzon is the largest. My hometown, Ballesteros, is in the province of Cagayan, on the northernmost tip of Luzon. The residents speak a language called Ilocano.

I knew there were places beyond my little world of Ballesteros because whenever I turned on the battery-operated radio, I heard programs coming from Taiwan and China.

Ballesteros is on my mind...

The West Philippine Sea on the edge of the town was the main attraction in Ballesteros. The residents went on picnics on the beach. My friends and I enjoyed playing and chasing each other on the sand. We also loved watching the sunset.

Many of the residents earned their living from fishing. Sometimes, in the afternoons, my siblings, cousins, and I helped the fishers haul in their huge nets. As reward, we were given a handful of their catch. I brought home my share for Grandaunt Inding to cook for dinner.

When the tides ebbed, small shellfish called *gakka* were left on the sand. Gakka could be found only in a few coastal towns of Cagayan. Fishers would wade into the waist-deep seawater and scoop the gakka out of the sand, using a basket with a bamboo handle called *tako*.

Cooking the gakka was simple. Boiling water was poured over the gakka and immediately drained. Then, the shells were ready to be opened.

Eating the shellfish was a kind of sport. Men popped a few pieces of gakka into their mouths, separated the meat with their teeth, then quickly spat out the shells. My friends and I watched the gakka eaters in amazement! We begged them to do the gakka show again and again!

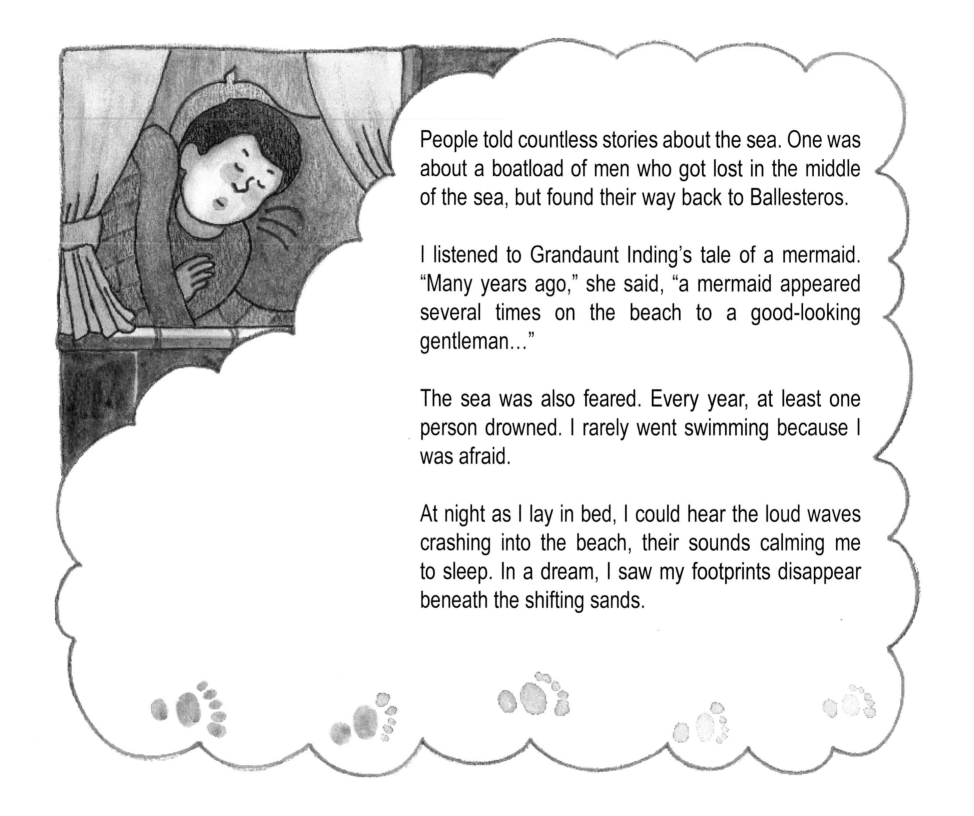

People told countless stories about the sea. One was about a boatload of men who got lost in the middle of the sea, but found their way back to Ballesteros.

I listened to Grandaunt Inding's tale of a mermaid. "Many years ago," she said, "a mermaid appeared several times on the beach to a good-looking gentleman…"

The sea was also feared. Every year, at least one person drowned. I rarely went swimming because I was afraid.

At night as I lay in bed, I could hear the loud waves crashing into the beach, their sounds calming me to sleep. In a dream, I saw my footprints disappear beneath the shifting sands.

Ballesteros is on my mind…

Our family lived in my Grandaunt Inding's nipa-roofed house in the *sentro*, the town center. The marketplace, bandstand, municipal hall, open-air auditorium, tennis court, and the Roman Catholic church were within walking distance of each other. There were two private high schools. One was on the south end, and the other on the east end.

Since there were only a few motor vehicles in Ballesteros, people were used to walking to their destinations in town. To go to the neighboring towns, they rode a jeepney, or a *kalesa*, a two-wheeled horse carriage. The ride was usually slow going. That was fine with me, especially when I rode the kalesa, because I loved looking at people and houses along the way.

Ballesteros had electricity for only a few hours at night. There was no television or telephone. However, there was a movie house that showed movies in the language Tagalog twice or thrice a week.

My friends and I played a lot. The whole town was our playground. We climbed trees and played hide-and-seek among the bushes. One game we particularly enjoyed was the *sungka*, played by two persons on a wooden board with holes on it. Each player had a *balay*, or house, to store the seashells used in the game. Whoever ended up with the most seashells in his or her balay was the winner.

Playtime usually ended before the church bells rang for evening prayers at 6 o'clock. We washed our hands very well before sitting down at the dinner table. When we ate, we used our bare hands. Steamed rice was served in every meal. Oftentimes, we had fish and vegetables.

Of the snacks we had, I loved the *patupat*. To make patupat, sticky rice was cooked in coconut milk. Then, the rice was shaped into a pyramid, wrapped in a banana leaf, and cooked slowly in an iron pot. Patupat was served with a dusting of sugar.

At Christmastime, I looked forward to eating the rice cake *tinubong*, made of sugar, sticky-rice flour, coconut milk, and grated young coconut meat. The mixture was placed inside a bamboo tube that was sealed on the open end with coconut husk or dried banana leaves. A rectangular hole was dug in the ground and filled with live charcoals, over which the tinubong was cooked.

When done, the bamboo tube was split open with a bolo, and the tinubong taken out and served.

On Thursdays, people waited with great excitement at a variety store. The bus driver from the city Manila delivered copies of the weekly magazine *Bannawag* (Dawn), written in Ilocano. People enjoyed reading comics, novels, and short stories. My friend Perlita asked, "Do you think the boy and the girl in the love story would meet again?" I answered, "*Mabalin*. Maybe." I thought, if they did not meet again, they would surely see each other in heaven. I had watched stories like that in Tagalog movies.

The town started honoring the dead on All Saints' Day. At 12 midnight of November 1st, people kept guard over their possessions because "spirits" might steal them. The next day, stolen goods, like ladders, cemetery crosses, and large earthen jars (called *burnay*), appeared at a street corner, where they were reclaimed by the owners. Although they were not pleased, the owners did not complain much because the "crime" was a tradition.

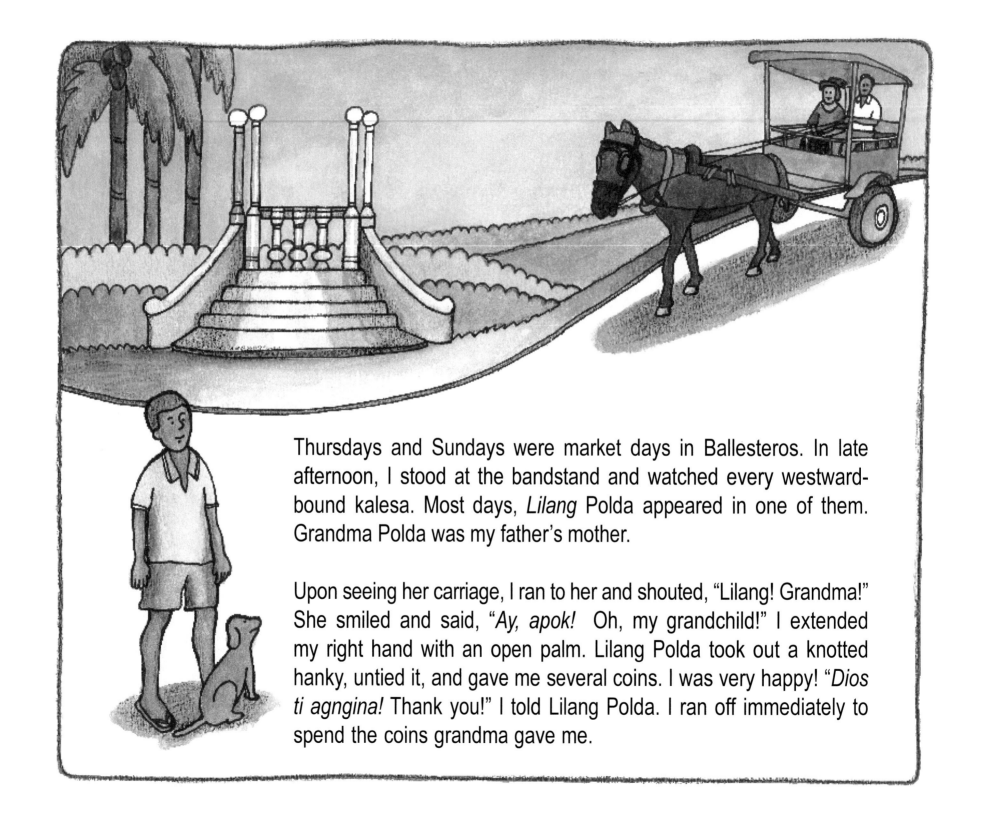

Thursdays and Sundays were market days in Ballesteros. In late afternoon, I stood at the bandstand and watched every westward-bound kalesa. Most days, *Lilang* Polda appeared in one of them. Grandma Polda was my father's mother.

Upon seeing her carriage, I ran to her and shouted, "Lilang! Grandma!" She smiled and said, "*Ay, apok!* Oh, my grandchild!" I extended my right hand with an open palm. Lilang Polda took out a knotted hanky, untied it, and gave me several coins. I was very happy! "*Dios ti agngina!* Thank you!" I told Lilang Polda. I ran off immediately to spend the coins grandma gave me.

My first job as a child was selling the newspaper *Manila Bulletin*. Granduncle Lope, the newspaper's distributor, recruited the neighborhood children to sell the *Bulletin*. I walked up and down the streets shouting, *"Bulletin! Bulletin! Bulletin!"* It was dusk by the time I finished the job. Granduncle Lope paid us only a few centavos, but we loved earning money!

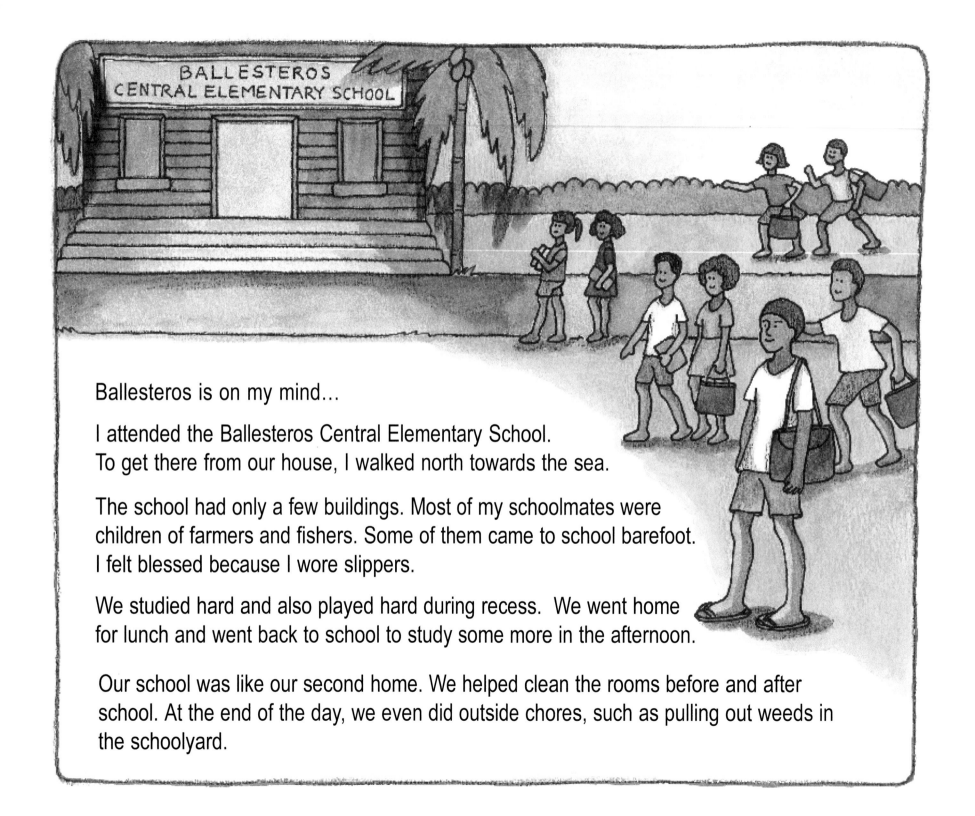

Ballesteros is on my mind...

I attended the Ballesteros Central Elementary School.
To get there from our house, I walked north towards the sea.

The school had only a few buildings. Most of my schoolmates were children of farmers and fishers. Some of them came to school barefoot. I felt blessed because I wore slippers.

We studied hard and also played hard during recess. We went home for lunch and went back to school to study some more in the afternoon.

Our school was like our second home. We helped clean the rooms before and after school. At the end of the day, we even did outside chores, such as pulling out weeds in the schoolyard.

A day in early January 1964 is one I cannot forget. Schoolchildren in Ballesteros were still on Christmas break. It was late afternoon when we heard shouts, "*Uram!* Fire!" Smoke could be seen from a distance. Word spread quickly that the elementary school was on fire. I ran towards the direction of my school! Embers were flying all over! I saw people climbing to the nipa rooftops of their houses and dousing them with water. A crowd had gathered in front of the school. I had never seen such a big fire in my life! It was scary! I stood motionless. I did not know what to do. The main school building burned to the ground right in front of my eyes. I knew immediately I would never step into my third-grade classroom again.

Nobody knew how the fire started. When we returned to school after the Christmas break, classrooms were set up in different homes. My classmates and I had our lessons on the second floor of a house assigned to our third-grade class. Our schooling was not interrupted at all.

Life went on as usual. At the end of the school year, the residents attended the school's closing ceremonies. When the names of the honor students were called, their proud parents came up the stage and pinned ribbons on them. The audience applauded loudly, and some members of the audience also went onstage to present gifts to the honor students. It was a big event.

In 1964, my family left Ballesteros to re-join father in Quezon City, a city next to Manila. However, my siblings and I returned to Ballesteros for our summer vacation. When I visited the school in 1966, I noticed that a new low-rise structure had replaced the big main building. I missed the old building that was made of wood and had concrete steps. One time, Miss Aquilizan, my second-grade teacher, asked two or three of my classmates to go up the steps and read aloud the huge sign that said: Ballesteros Central Elementary School.

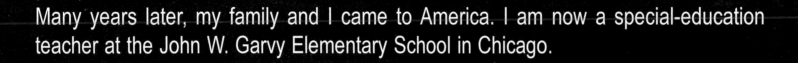

Many years later, my family and I came to America. I am now a special-education teacher at the John W. Garvy Elementary School in Chicago.

Whenever I get a chance, I tell my students stories of my wonderful childhood in Ballesteros. They are interested in knowing more about Ballesteros. I have taught them how to play the sungka, the game I enjoyed playing as a child, and have shown them pictures of gakka.

I remember people, places, and events in Ballesteros as if they happened only yesterday. Sometimes I feel like I can still breathe the salty breeze of the sea and hear the whooshing sound of water rushing to the beach. I see my Lilang Polda getting off the kalesa… my friends calling me to play, "Rey! Rey! Rey!"

Ballesteros is on my mind…

GLOSSARY*

Ay, apok	(ai AH-pohk)	Oh, my grandchild
Balay	(bah-LAI)	House; also a place for storing seashells in the board game *sungka*
Bannawag	(bahn-NAH-wahg)	Weekly magazine written in Ilocano
Burnay	(boor-NAI)	Large earthen jar
Dios ti agngina	(DEEYOS tee ahg-NGEE-nah)	Thank you

*The capitalized syllable is stressed in pronunciation.

To pronounce the letter *ng* in the Filipino alphabet, say *ring* in your head but just vocalize the last *ng* in the word.

 # GLOSSARY*

Gakka	(GAHK-kah)	Seashell found in Ballesteros, Cagayan
Kalesa	(kah-LEH-sah)	Two-wheeled horse carriage
Lilang	(LEE-lahng)	Grandma
Mabalin	(mah-bah-LEEN)	Maybe
Patupat	(pah-TOO-paht)	Rice cake shaped into a pyramid and wrapped in a banana leaf

*The capitalized syllable is stressed in pronunciation.

To pronounce the letter *ng* in the Filipino alphabet, say *ring* in your head but just vocalize the last *ng* in the word.

 GLOSSARY*

Sentro	(SEHN-troh)	Town center
Sungka	(SOONG-kah)	Board game played with seashells by two players
Tako	(TAH-koh)	Basket with bamboo handle to scoop *gakka* out of the sand
Tinubong	(tee-NOO-bohng)	Rice cake cooked in a bamboo tube
Uram	(OO-rahm)	Fire

*The capitalized syllable is stressed in pronunciation.

To pronounce the letter *ng* in the Filipino alphabet, say *ring* in your head but just vocalize the last *ng* in the word.

Rey E. de la Cruz, Ed.D., started writing and directing plays when he was in high school. At 17, he won third prize in the Carlos Palanca Memorial Awards for Literature 1972, the Philippines' most prestigious literary awards, for *Kombensiyon ng mga Halimaw* (Monsters' Convention), a satire on the Philippine Constitutional Convention. He is an avid traveler, and enjoys films, plays, and books. Because his imagination was nurtured in Ballesteros, he has always been fascinated by small-town stories. He lives in Glenview, Illinois.

Tenni Magcase is a visual artist, portrait painter, and illustrator of children's books. Her vibrant illustration in *The Magic Jeepney* earned her a place as a finalist in the Noma Concours for Picture Book Illustrations 1982, organized by the Asia/Pacific Cultural Centre for UNESCO. A resident of Morris Plains, New Jersey, she was a former president of the New York-based Society of Philippine American Artists.